BIG BOOK
OF VIOLIN & CELLO DUETS

34 Pop Songs, Movie Hits, and Classic Standards including
Beauty and the Beast • City of Stars • Hallelujah • Imagine
Moon River • Perfect • Shallow • Tears in Heaven
What a Wonderful World • You Raise Me Up
and more!

HAL•LEONARD®

BIG BOOK
OF VIOLIN & CELLO DUETS

Arranged by Fulvia Mancini and Massimiliano Martinelli

2	Beauty and the Beast	44	Mamma Mia
4	Bohemian Rhapsody	46	Moon River
7	Candle in the Wind	48	My Favorite Things
10	Cast Your Fate to the Wind	39	My Heart Will Go On (Love Theme from 'Titanic')
12	City of Stars	50	Perfect
16	Defying Gravity	52	Rewrite the Stars
20	(Everything I Do) I Do It for You	54	Shallow
22	Fly Me to the Moon (In Other Words)	78	Someone Like You
24	Hallelujah	58	The Sound of Silence
26	Happy	60	Tears in Heaven
28	How Far I'll Go	62	Viva La Vida
30	I Dreamed a Dream	66	The Way You Look Tonight
32	Imagine	68	What a Wonderful World
19	Lean on Me	70	What Makes You Beautiful
34	Let It Be	72	When I'm Sixty-Four
36	Let It Go	74	You Raise Me Up
42	Love Story	76	Your Song

ISBN 978-1-70514-115-1

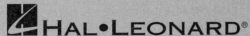

HAL•LEONARD®

Visit Hal Leonard Online at
www.halleonard.com

Contact us:
Hal Leonard
7777 West Bluemound Road
Milwaukee, WI 53213
Email: info@halleonard.com

In Europe, contact:
Hal Leonard Europe Limited
42 Wigmore Street
Marylebone, London, W1U 2RN
Email: info@halleonardeurope.com

In Australia, contact:
Hal Leonard Australia Pty. Ltd.
4 Lentara Court
Cheltenham, Victoria, 3192 Australia
Email: info@halleonard.com.au

BEAUTY AND THE BEAST

from BEAUTY AND THE BEAST

Music by ALAN MENKEN
Lyrics by HOWARD ASHMAN

BOHEMIAN RHAPSODY

Words and Music by
FREDDIE MERCURY

5

CANDLE IN THE WIND

Words and Music by ELTON JOHN
and BERNIE TAUPIN

CAST YOUR FATE TO THE WIND

Music by VINCE GUARALDI

CITY OF STARS

from LA LA LAND

Music by JUSTIN HURWITZ
Lyrics by BENJ PASEK & JUSTIN PAUL

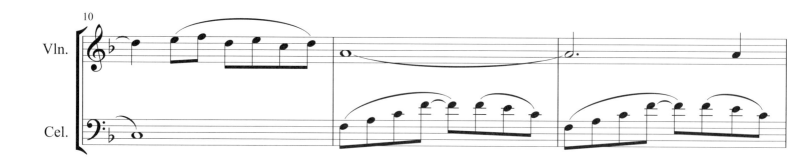

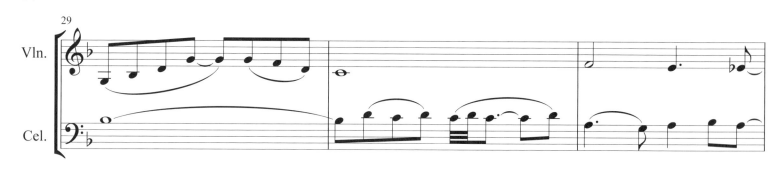

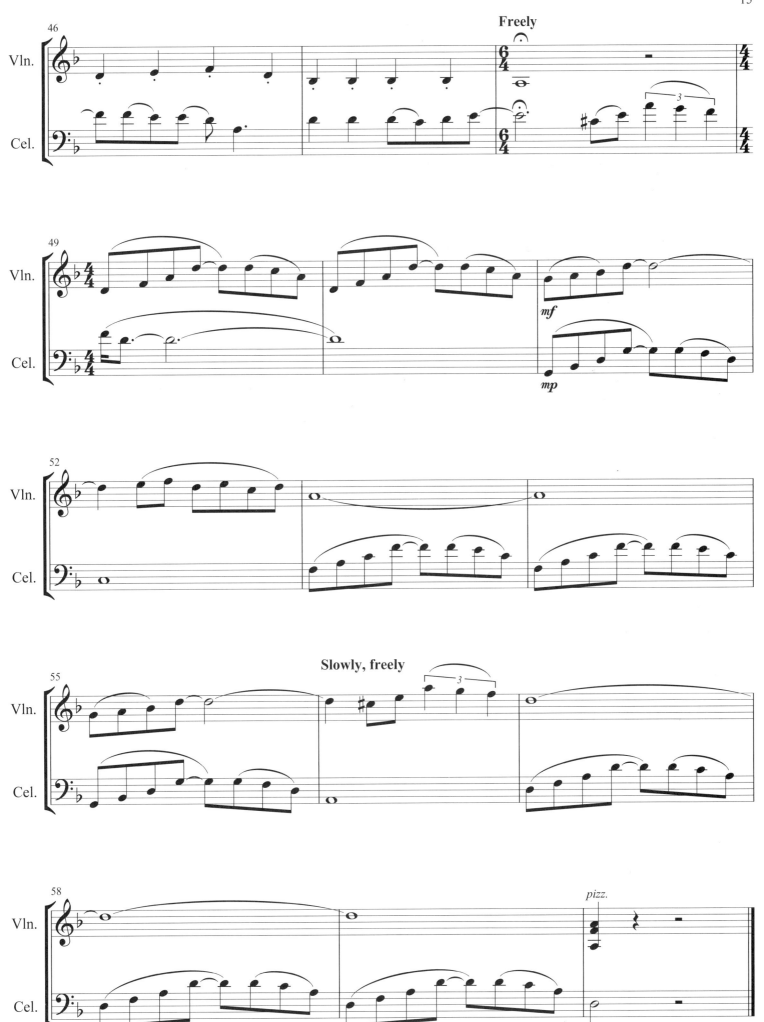

DEFYING GRAVITY
from the Broadway Musical WICKED

Music and Lyrics by
STEPHEN SCHWARTZ

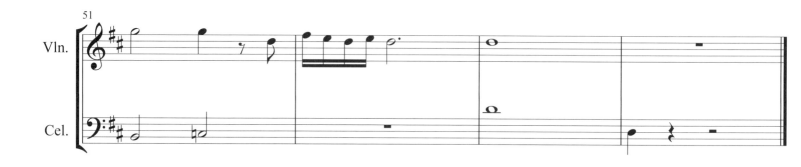

LEAN ON ME

Words and Music by
BILL WITHERS

(Everything I Do)
I DO IT FOR YOU

from the Motion Picture ROBIN HOOD: PRINCE OF THIEVES

Words and Music by BRYAN ADAMS,
R.J. LANGE and MICHAEL KAMEN

FLY ME TO THE MOON
(In Other Words)

Words and Music by
BART HOWARD

HALLELUJAH

Words and Music by
LEONARD COHEN

HAPPY
from DESPICABLE ME 2

Words and Music by
PHARRELL WILLIAMS

HOW FAR I'LL GO

from MOANA

Music and Lyrics by
LIN-MANUEL MIRANDA

I DREAMED A DREAM

from LES MISÉRABLES

Music by CLAUDE-MICHEL SCHÖNBERG
Lyrics by ALAIN BOUBLIL,
JEAN-MARC NATEL and HERBERT KRETZMER

IMAGINE

Words and Music by
JOHN LENNON

LET IT BE

Words and Music by JOHN LENNON
and PAUL McCARTNEY

LET IT GO
from FROZEN

Music and Lyrics by KRISTEN ANDERSON-LOPEZ
and ROBERT LOPEZ

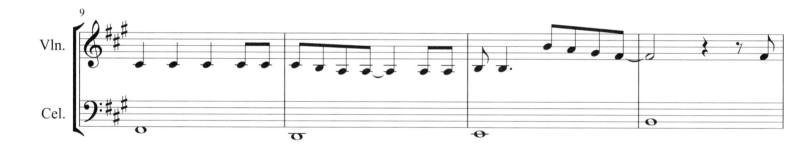

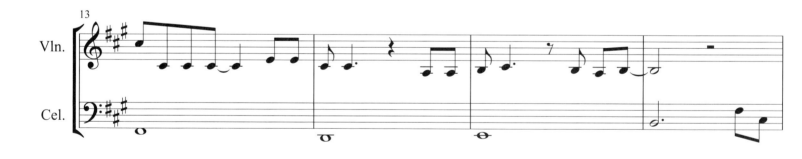

MY HEART WILL GO ON
(Love Theme From 'Titanic')
from the Paramount and Twentieth Century Fox Motion Picture TITANIC

Music by JAMES HORNER
Lyric by WILL JENNINGS

LOVE STORY

Words and Music by
TAYLOR SWIFT

MAMMA MIA

Words and Music by BENNY ANDERSSON,
BJÖRN ULVAEUS and STIG ANDERSON

MOON RIVER

from the Paramount Picture BREAKFAST AT TIFFANY'S

Words by JOHNNY MERCER
Music by HENRY MANCINI

MY FAVORITE THINGS
from THE SOUND OF MUSIC

Lyrics by OSCAR HAMMERSTEIN II
Music by RICHARD RODGERS

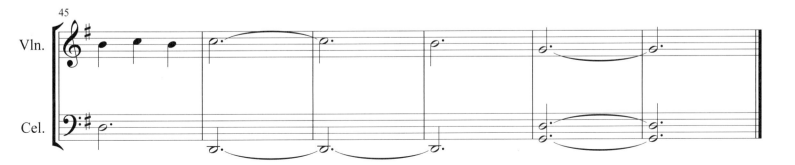

PERFECT

Words and Music by
ED SHEERAN

Classic Ballad

REWRITE THE STARS

from THE GREATEST SHOWMAN

Words and Music by BENJ PASEK
and JUSTIN PAUL

SHALLOW

from A STAR IS BORN

Words and Music by STEFANI GERMANOTTA,
MARK RONSON, ANDREW WYATT
and ANTHONY ROSSOMANDO

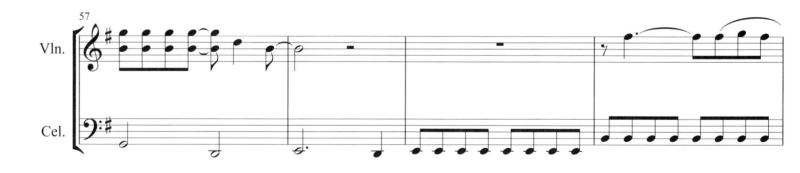

THE SOUND OF SILENCE

Words and Music by
PAUL SIMON

TEARS IN HEAVEN

Words and Music by ERIC CLAPTON
and WILL JENNINGS

VIVA LA VIDA

Words and Music by GUY BERRYMAN,
JON BUCKLAND, WILL CHAMPION
and CHRIS MARTIN

64

THE WAY YOU LOOK TONIGHT

Words by DOROTHY FIELDS
Music by JEROME KERN

WHAT A WONDERFUL WORLD

Words and Music by GEORGE DAVID WEISS
and BOB THIELE

WHAT MAKES YOU BEAUTIFUL

Words and Music by SAVAN KOTECHA,
RAMI YACOUB and CARL FALK

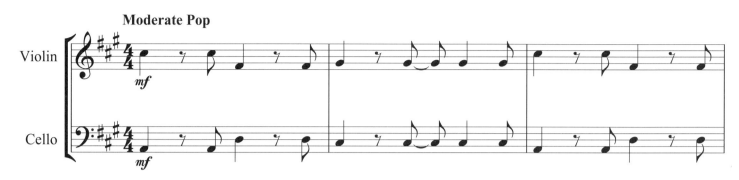

WHEN I'M SIXTY-FOUR

Words and Music by JOHN LENNON
and PAUL McCARTNEY

YOU RAISE ME UP

Words and Music by BRENDAN GRAHAM
and ROLF LOVLAND

YOUR SONG

Words and Music by ELTON JOHN
and BERNIE TAUPIN

77

SOMEONE LIKE YOU

Words and Music by ADELE ADKINS
and DAN WILSON

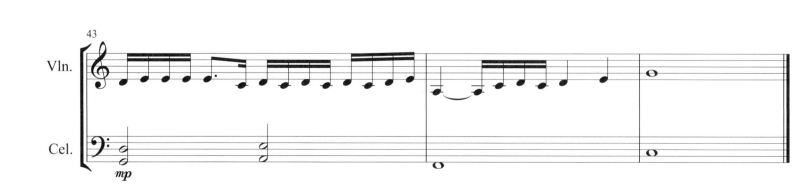

VIOLIN

BIG BOOK
OF VIOLIN & CELLO DUETS

Arranged by Fulvia Mancini and Massimiliano Martinelli

2 Beauty and the Beast

4 Bohemian Rhapsody

6 Candle in the Wind

3 Cast Your Fate to the Wind

8 City of Stars

10 Defying Gravity

12 (Everything I Do)
   I Do It for You

13 Fly Me to the Moon
   (In Other Words)

14 Hallelujah

15 Happy

16 How Far I'll Go

18 I Dreamed a Dream

20 Imagine

17 Lean on Me

22 Let It Be

24 Let It Go

26 Love Story

27 Mamma Mia

28 Moon River

29 My Favorite Things

30 My Heart Will Go On
   (Love Theme from 'Titanic')

32 Perfect

34 Rewrite the Stars

36 Shallow

38 Someone Like You

33 The Sound of Silence

40 Tears in Heaven

42 Viva La Vida

41 The Way You Look Tonight

44 What a Wonderful World

45 What Makes You Beautiful

46 When I'm Sixty-Four

47 You Raise Me Up

48 Your Song

ISBN 978-1-70514-115-1

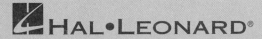

HAL•LEONARD®

Visit Hal Leonard Online at
www.halleonard.com

Contact us:
Hal Leonard
7777 West Bluemound Road
Milwaukee, WI 53213
Email: info@halleonard.com

In Europe, contact:
Hal Leonard Europe Limited
42 Wigmore Street
Marylebone, London, W1U 2RN
Email: info@halleonardeurope.com

In Australia, contact:
Hal Leonard Australia Pty. Ltd.
4 Lentara Court
Cheltenham, Victoria, 3192 Australia
Email: info@halleonard.com.au

00368212

2

BEAUTY AND THE BEAST

from BEAUTY AND THE BEAST

Violin

Music by ALAN MENKEN
Lyrics by HOWARD ASHMAN

CAST YOUR FATE TO THE WIND

Violin

Music by VINCE GUARALDI

BOHEMIAN RHAPSODY

Violin

Words and Music by
FREDDIE MERCURY

5

CANDLE IN THE WIND

Violin

Words and Music by ELTON JOHN
and BERNIE TAUPIN

CITY OF STARS
from LA LA LAND

Violin

Music by JUSTIN HURWITZ
Lyrics by BENJ PASEK & JUSTIN PAUL

DEFYING GRAVITY
from the Broadway Musical WICKED

Violin

Music and Lyrics by
STEPHEN SCHWARTZ

(Everything I Do)
I DO IT FOR YOU

from the Motion Picture ROBIN HOOD: PRINCE OF THIEVES

Violin

Words and Music by BRYAN ADAMS,
R.J. LANGE and MICHAEL KAMEN

FLY ME TO THE MOON
(In Other Words)

Violin

Words and Music by
BART HOWARD

HALLELUJAH

Violin

Words and Music by
LEONARD COHEN

HAPPY
from DESPICABLE ME 2

Words and Music by
PHARRELL WILLIAMS

Violin

HOW FAR I'LL GO

from MOANA

Violin

Music and Lyrics by
LIN-MANUEL MIRANDA

LEAN ON ME

Violin

Words and Music by
BILL WITHERS

I DREAMED A DREAM
from LES MISÉRABLES

Violin

Music by CLAUDE-MICHEL SCHÖNBERG
Lyrics by ALAIN BOUBLIL,
JEAN-MARC NATEL and HERBERT KRETZMER

19

IMAGINE

Violin

Words and Music by
JOHN LENNON

LET IT BE

Violin

Words and Music by JOHN LENNON
and PAUL McCARTNEY

LET IT GO
from FROZEN

Violin

Music and Lyrics by KRISTEN ANDERSON-LOPEZ
and ROBERT LOPEZ

LOVE STORY

Violin

Words and Music by
TAYLOR SWIFT

MAMMA MIA

Violin

Words and Music by BENNY ANDERSSON,
BJÖRN ULVAEUS and STIG ANDERSON

MOON RIVER

from the Paramount Picture BREAKFAST AT TIFFANY'S

Violin

Words by JOHNNY MERCER
Music by HENRY MANCINI

MY FAVORITE THINGS

from THE SOUND OF MUSIC

Violin

Lyrics by OSCAR HAMMERSTEIN II
Music by RICHARD RODGERS

MY HEART WILL GO ON
(Love Theme From 'Titanic')
from the Paramount and Twentieth Century Fox Motion Picture TITANIC

Violin

Music by JAMES HORNER
Lyric by WILL JENNINGS

PERFECT

Violin

Words and Music by
ED SHEERAN

THE SOUND OF SILENCE

Violin

Words and Music by
PAUL SIMON

REWRITE THE STARS

from THE GREATEST SHOWMAN

Violin

Words and Music by BENJ PASEK
and JUSTIN PAUL

rit.

SHALLOW
from A STAR IS BORN

Violin

Words and Music by STEFANI GERMANOTTA,
MARK RONSON, ANDREW WYATT
and ANTHONY ROSSOMANDO

SOMEONE LIKE YOU

Violin

Words and Music by ADELE ADKINS
and DAN WILSON

TEARS IN HEAVEN

Violin

Words and Music by ERIC CLAPTON
and WILL JENNINGS

THE WAY YOU LOOK TONIGHT

Words by DOROTHY FIELDS
Music by JEROME KERN

Violin

VIVA LA VIDA

Violin

Words and Music by GUY BERRYMAN,
JON BUCKLAND, WILL CHAMPION
and CHRIS MARTIN

WHAT A WONDERFUL WORLD

Violin

Words and Music by GEORGE DAVID WEISS
and BOB THIELE

WHAT MAKES YOU BEAUTIFUL

Violin

Words and Music by SAVAN KOTECHA,
RAMI YACOUB and CARL FALK

WHEN I'M SIXTY-FOUR

Violin

Words and Music by JOHN LENNON
and PAUL McCARTNEY

YOU RAISE ME UP

Violin

Words and Music by BRENDAN GRAHAM
and ROLF LOVLAND

YOUR SONG

Violin

Words and Music by ELTON JOHN
and BERNIE TAUPIN

CELLO
BIG BOOK
OF VIOLIN & CELLO DUETS
Arranged by Fulvia Mancini and Massimiliano Martinelli

2 Beauty and the Beast

4 Bohemian Rhapsody

6 Candle in the Wind

3 Cast Your Fate to the Wind

8 City of Stars

10 Defying Gravity

12 (Everything I Do)
I Do It for You

13 Fly Me to the Moon
(In Other Words)

14 Hallelujah

15 Happy

16 How Far I'll Go

18 I Dreamed a Dream

20 Imagine

17 Lean on Me

22 Let It Be

24 Let It Go

26 Love Story

27 Mamma Mia

28 Moon River

29 My Favorite Things

30 My Heart Will Go On
(Love Theme from 'Titanic')

32 Perfect

34 Rewrite the Stars

36 Shallow

38 Someone Like You

33 The Sound of Silence

40 Tears in Heaven

42 Viva La Vida

41 The Way You Look Tonight

44 What a Wonderful World

45 What Makes You Beautiful

46 When I'm Sixty-Four

47 You Raise Me Up

48 Your Song

ISBN 978-1-70514-115-1

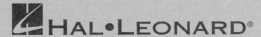

HAL•LEONARD®

Visit Hal Leonard Online at
www.halleonard.com

Contact us:
Hal Leonard
7777 West Bluemound Road
Milwaukee, WI 53213
Email: info@halleonard.com

In Europe, contact:
Hal Leonard Europe Limited
42 Wigmore Street
Marylebone, London, W1U 2RN
Email: info@halleonardeurope.com

In Australia, contact:
Hal Leonard Australia Pty. Ltd.
4 Lentara Court
Cheltenham, Victoria, 3192 Australia
Email: info@halleonard.com.au

BEAUTY AND THE BEAST
from BEAUTY AND THE BEAST

Cello

Music by ALAN MENKEN
Lyrics by HOWARD ASHMAN

CAST YOUR FATE TO THE WIND

Cello

Music by VINCE GUARALDI

4

BOHEMIAN RHAPSODY

Cello

Words and Music by
FREDDIE MERCURY

5

CANDLE IN THE WIND

Cello

Words and Music by ELTON JOHN
and BERNIE TAUPIN

CITY OF STARS
from LA LA LAND

Cello

Music by JUSTIN HURWITZ
Lyrics by BENJ PASEK & JUSTIN PAUL

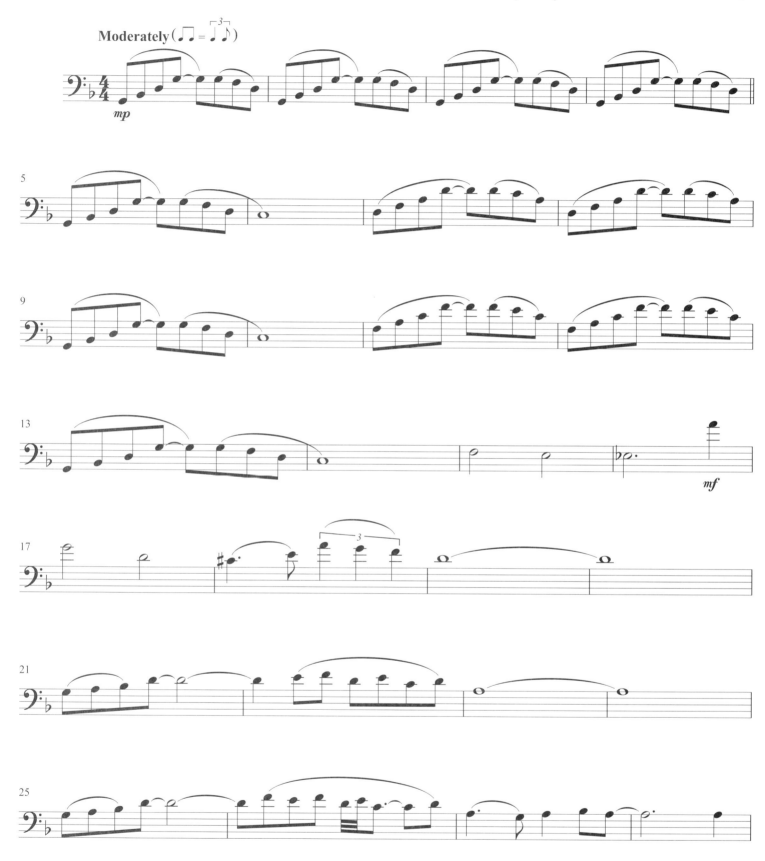

DEFYING GRAVITY
from the Broadway Musical WICKED

Cello

Music and Lyrics by
STEPHEN SCHWARTZ

(Everything I Do)
I DO IT FOR YOU
from the Motion Picture ROBIN HOOD: PRINCE OF THIEVES

Cello

Words and Music by BRYAN ADAMS,
R.J. LANGE and MICHAEL KAMEN

FLY ME TO THE MOON
(In Other Words)

Cello

Words and Music by
BART HOWARD

HALLELUJAH

Cello

Words and Music by
LEONARD COHEN

HAPPY
from DESPICABLE ME 2

Words and Music by
PHARRELL WILLIAMS

Cello

HOW FAR I'LL GO

from MOANA

Cello

Music and Lyrics by
LIN-MANUEL MIRANDA

LEAN ON ME

Cello

Words and Music by
BILL WITHERS

I DREAMED A DREAM
from LES MISÉRABLES

Cello

Music by CLAUDE-MICHEL SCHÖNBERG
Lyrics by ALAIN BOUBLIL,
JEAN-MARC NATEL and HERBERT KRETZMER

IMAGINE

Cello

Words and Music by
JOHN LENNON

LET IT BE

Cello

Words and Music by JOHN LENNON
and PAUL McCARTNEY

LET IT GO
from FROZEN

Cello

Music and Lyrics by KRISTEN ANDERSON-LOPEZ
and ROBERT LOPEZ

Half-time feel, mysterious

LOVE STORY

Cello

Words and Music by
TAYLOR SWIFT

MAMMA MIA

Cello

Words and Music by BENNY ANDERSSON,
BJÖRN ULVAEUS and STIG ANDERSON

MOON RIVER
from the Paramount Picture BREAKFAST AT TIFFANY'S

Cello

Words by JOHNNY MERCER
Music by HENRY MANCINI

MY FAVORITE THINGS
from THE SOUND OF MUSIC

Cello

Lyrics by OSCAR HAMMERSTEIN II
Music by RICHARD RODGERS

MY HEART WILL GO ON
(Love Theme From 'Titanic')
from the Paramount and Twentieth Century Fox Motion Picture TITANIC

Cello

Music by JAMES HORNER
Lyric by WILL JENNINGS

32

PERFECT

Cello

Words and Music by
ED SHEERAN

THE SOUND OF SILENCE

Cello

Words and Music by
PAUL SIMON

REWRITE THE STARS
from THE GREATEST SHOWMAN

Cello

Words and Music by BENJ PASEK
and JUSTIN PAUL

SHALLOW
from A STAR IS BORN

Cello

Words and Music by STEFANI GERMANOTTA,
MARK RONSON, ANDREW WYATT
and ANTHONY ROSSOMANDO

SOMEONE LIKE YOU

Cello

Words and Music by ADELE ADKINS
and DAN WILSON

Ballad

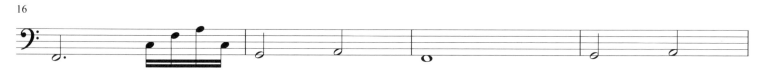

TEARS IN HEAVEN

Cello

Words and Music by ERIC CLAPTON
and WILL JENNINGS

THE WAY YOU LOOK TONIGHT

Cello

Words by DOROTHY FIELDS
Music by JEROME KERN

VIVA LA VIDA

Cello

Words and Music by GUY BERRYMAN,
JON BUCKLAND, WILL CHAMPION
and CHRIS MARTIN

WHAT A WONDERFUL WORLD

Cello

Words and Music by GEORGE DAVID WEISS
and BOB THIELE

WHAT MAKES YOU BEAUTIFUL

Cello

Words and Music by SAVAN KOTECHA,
RAMI YACOUB and CARL FALK

WHEN I'M SIXTY-FOUR

Cello

Words and Music by JOHN LENNON
and PAUL McCARTNEY

YOU RAISE ME UP

Cello

Words and Music by BRENDAN GRAHAM
and ROLF LOVLAND

YOUR SONG

Cello

Words and Music by ELTON JOHN
and BERNIE TAUPIN